A Legend of Fyvie Castle. By K. G. [i.e. Catherine J. B. Gordon.]

K. G., Catherine Jane, Bradby Gordon

A Legend of Fyvie Castle. By K. G. [i.e. Catherine J. B. Gordon.]
G., K.
British Library, Historical Print Editions
British Library
Gordon, Catherine Jane, Bradby
1870?]
77 p. ; 8º.
12630.p.4.

The BiblioLife Network

This project was made possible in part by the BiblioLife Network (BLN), a project aimed at addressing some of the huge challenges facing book preservationists around the world. The BLN includes libraries, library networks, archives, subject matter experts, online communities and library service providers. We believe every book ever published should be available as a high-quality print reproduction; printed on- demand anywhere in the world. This insures the ongoing accessibility of the content and helps generate sustainable revenue for the libraries and organizations that work to preserve these important materials.

The following book is in the "public domain" and represents an authentic reproduction of the text as printed by the original publisher. While we have attempted to accurately maintain the integrity of the original work, there are sometimes problems with the original book or micro-film from which the books were digitized. This can result in minor errors in reproduction. Possible imperfections include missing and blurred pages, poor pictures, markings and other reproduction issues beyond our control. Because this work is culturally important, we have made it available as part of our commitment to protecting, preserving, and promoting the world's literature.

GUIDE TO FOLD-OUTS, MAPS and OVERSIZED IMAGES

In an online database, page images do not need to conform to the size restrictions found in a printed book. When converting these images back into a printed bound book, the page sizes are standardized in ways that maintain the detail of the original. For large images, such as fold-out maps, the original page image is split into two or more pages.

Guidelines used to determine the split of oversize pages:

- Some images are split vertically; large images require vertical and horizontal splits.
- For horizontal splits, the content is split left to right.
- For vertical splits, the content is split from top to bottom.
- For both vertical and horizontal splits, the image is processed from top left to bottom right.

1296 Edward 1st slept at Fyvie "

1325. Mentioned as "Kings Park of Fyvie" a Royal Residence of Robert the Bruce

1370 Given by Robert 2nd to his son & (afterwards Robert 3rd) & by him to

1386 Sir James Lindsay — besieged by Robert de Keith & defended by Lady Lindsay until relieved by her husband

1390 Acquired by Sir Henry Preston in exchange for Ralph Percy whom Sir Henry had taken prisoner at the battle of Otterburne

1433 Sir George Meldrum succeeded in right of his wife & daughter of Sir Henry Preston

1596 Purchased of the Meldrums by Sir Alexander Seton afterwards created 1st Lord Fyvie & subsequently 1st Earl of Dunfermline

1644 Montrose took up his quarters in the Castle on the 28th Octr & fought Argyle a few days after in the immediate vicinity of the Castle. He was successful notwithstanding he had a much smaller force & was ill supplied with ammunition

into bullets every Pewter dish, & ev[e]n 1 flagon" his entrenchments still remain

1690 — James 4th Earl of Dunfermline outlawed, he followed James 2nd to France after the battle of Killiecrankie He died at St Germains 1694 he married Jane sister of the 1st Duke of Gordon —

1726 Came into possession of Wm 2nd Earl of Aberdeen settled on his 3rd Wife Anne daughter of 2nd Duke of Gordon sister of Lord Lewis Gordon & her heirs —

A LEGEND
FYVIE CASTLE

1847 — Wm Cosmo Gordon Gt Grandson of 2nd Earl of Aberdeen & Anne daughter & Sister Gordon

A Legend

of

Fyvie Castle.

BY

K. G.

"CASTETH SCRIBBLE"

For Private Circulation.

COPYRIGHT RESERVED

Introduction.

SOME of the incidents of the following legend have been long familiar to the inhabitants of Fyvie and its neighbourhood; but an additional interest was imparted to them in the spring of 1867, when, on the removal of a portion of the wainscot of the drawing-room of the old Castle, there was discovered a small altar, and in one of the divisions a secret drawer, the inspection of whose contents kindled in the mind of the writer a renewed curiosity, and awakened a desire to give expression, in her own language, in a connected narrative, to the several incidents of the interesting history. It would impart no additional interest to the story to add that a manuscript was found, yellow with age, and that the handwriting was bold and legible, or in smaller and delicate characters, such as might have been traced by a female hand—the present writer having been intent only on giving to those of her friends who may care to read it a modernized version of the "Legend of Fyvie Castle."

The following description of the "Old Castle," principally taken from Billings' work on Scottish architecture may be interesting to the reader.

"Fyvie Castle is one of the noblest and most beautiful specimens of the French architecture, as introduced into Scotland in the reign of James VI. by the Scottish barons. Its four princely towers, with their luxuriant coronet of coned turrets, sharp gables, tall roofs and chimneys, canopied dormer windows and rude statuary, present a sky outline at once graceful, rich, and massive. The central or clock tower, consists in appearance of two semi-round towers, with a deep curtain between them, retired within a round arched recess of peculiar height and depth. The minor departments of the building are profusely decorated with mouldings, crockets, canopies, and statuary. The interior is in the same fine keeping with the exterior. The great staircase is an architectural triumph such as few mansions can exhibit; and it is so broad and gently graduated as to justify a traditional boast that the Laird's horse used to ascend it. In the Meldrum tower is contained a secret and, for many years, unopened chamber, which was supposed by some persons to contain treasure, by others to be the abode of evil spirits!"

Fyvie Castle holds a humble but popular

place in poetry, as associated with the loves of its valiant trumpeter and "Mill o' Tiftie's Annie." The well-known ballad tells us that—

> "At Mill o' Tiftie lived a man,
>   Upon the lands of Fyvie;
> He had a lovely daughter fair,
>   And she was bonnie Annie.
>
> Lord Fyvie had a trumpeter
>   Whose name was Andrew Lammie;
> He had the art to win the heart
>   Of Mill o' Tiftie's Annie."

Faithful to the poetic legend, the figure of the trumpeter, starting in stone from the peak of a turret, points his constant but silent trumpet towards the dwelling of the inexorable miller. Tiftie's Annie was no imaginary person; her tombstone is in Fyvie kirkyard, and documents show that her father was owner of the mill in 1672.

A Legend of Fyvie Castle.

"Such omens in the place, there seemed to be
  At every crooked turn, or on the landing,
The straining eyeball was prepared to see
  Some Apparition standing.

O'er all there hung a shadow and a fear;
  A sense of mystery the spirit daunted,
And said as plain as whisper in the ear,
  The place is Haunted!"

SOMETIME towards the end of the seventeenth century a family of the name of Gray lived at Tifty, a farm on the Fyvie property. Robert, the father, always of a very stern disposition, had, since the death of his wife—which event occurred some years earlier than the time of which we are now speaking—changed considerably, and had become still more overbearing and exacting; so that his children were somewhat afraid of him, and were compelled to yield him unquestioning obedience. It seemed almost as if all the softer and gentler feelings of his nature had been interred in the grave of his wife.

His family, consisting of three sons and a daughter, were all residing at home; the sons being employed in the various occupations incidental to agricultural life. They had all received a good education relative to their social condition; and Steenie, the youngest son, stimulated by the desire of becoming first a schoolmaster and subsequently a minister continued still to study at every available opportunity—affording an illustration, among many others, of a laudable emulation and tenacity of purpose which have, in not a few instances, been instrumental in winning for his countrymen a high and noble reputation.

A special feeling of affection existed between Steenie and his sister; he was always ready to do any thing for her. They were nearly of an age, and often pursued their studies and pleasures together.

In stature, figure, and presence, nature had abundantly favoured Jessie Gray. Of average height, her graceful and slender form gave her the appearance of being taller; of fair complexion, and with a delicate colour on her cheeks, that increased in depth when any excitement called forth warmth of feeling; with deep violet eyes and dark brown hair, which, most unusual in girls at that time, curled in thick ringlets round her small well-shaped head, she was indeed a lovely girl, such an one as the poet, kindling with emotion and rapt in admiration of her almost ethereal beauty, might in imagination have beheld when pouring forth those exquisite lines:—

> " And on that cheek, and o'er that brow
>   So soft, so calm, yet eloquent.
> The smiles that win, the tints that glow,
>   But tell of days in goodness spent.
> A mind at peace with all below,
>   A heart whose love is innocent."

And she was gentle and good as she was pretty; her father and brothers doted on her, and were naturally proud of her. Her time was almost fully occupied in making their home comfortable and in doing the necessary needlework of the family; and as they kept a servant for household work, Jessie had some little spare time to roam in the pretty woods of Fyvie. Nothing pleased her more than to take her work or a book and sally forth on a ramble, sometimes to seek for pearls, of which there were plenty in the Ythan.

On one of these occasions she was suddenly

startled by the report of a gun, and, missing her footing, she fell into the river, and the stones being smooth and slippery, she could not easily regain her feet. She unconsciously gave a slight scream, although unaware that there was anyone near; but upon hearing which a young man sprang from the opposite bank, and without much difficulty soon rescued her from her uncomfortable position.

As she stood, a little alarmed, her garments wet and dripping from her late immersion, her cheek heightened in beauty by the slight degree of confusion which she was feeling, she might have appeared to her deliverer as the beautiful Naiad of the stream from which she had just emerged; and surely few could have censured him, if, as in realization of the exquisite tales of a remote age, he had at once offered up his homage and his devotion at her shrine. She soon recovered her self-possession, and in earnest and ingenuous terms thanked the youth for his prompt assistance, and having done this, moved slowly away towards her home.

Whether from a feeling of duty only, or from a desire to know more of the fair being whom he had thus assisted, or from the impulse of some deeper emotion felt, but perhaps not acknowledged even to himself, he instinctively followed and accompanied her to her father's house, telling her on the way his name and place of abode.

William Lyndsay—for such was the young man's name—had lately come to live at Fyvie, near to the Castle, the proprietor of which had given him employment in a variety of occupations, not of a laborious character, nor such as to engross the whole of his time.

This was so far fortunate for him in that, as he possessed considerable intelligence, with a desire for further improvement, he had thus opportunities of obtaining, unaided, much additional knowledge, whose acquisition was greatly facilitated by the free use of the books in the library of the Castle, and also by an early good education, valuable and superior then as now, and perhaps such as no other nation affords to its industrial population; an exception honourable to the sagacity, the benevolence, and the philanthropy of Scotia's richer sons.

Would that their example might appeal to the Southron, and awaken in his mind a deep sense of the responsibility resting on the wealthiest and most prosperous nation of the world, where there are, unhappily, still to be found seething masses of ignorance and its offspring of poverty and crime.

But having rescued our heroine, we must not forget her altogether. Jessie was in no way the worse for her accident, at least bodily. She did not mention it to any one except to her brother

Steenie, who was at home when she returned. Having heard her account of her misadventure, and of her obligations to William Lyndsay, he received the latter very cordially, expressed his pleasure at the opportunity thus afforded of making his acquaintance, and after some short and unimportant conversation, Jessie Gray and William Lyndsay parted.

They parted! Aye! and from that hour there came up slowly from the horizon of their existence a small cloud, destined either to grow in beauty and be gilded by the bright rays of the sun of a life's happiness, or it might be to increase in darkness and in gloom, and overshadow with a sorrow blacker than despair the bright hopes of these young and trusting hearts.

William Lyndsay returned slowly to his home. A new and undefined feeling had taken possession of him; he whistled his familiar airs; he sang snatches of his native songs; but behind the whistling and behind the singing, deep in the inner mind, an image had found a shrine, from which there seemed not to be the power, had there been the wish, to remove it. The vision of Jessie Gray still rose up before him, and his meditative mood was encouraged by the softening and subduing influence of a heavenly, calm, moonlight evening, the placid surface of the lake, the sweet and soft monotony of its lapping wavelets, and the almost universal quiet that reigned around. In anticipation he had fully realized the beautiful picture of the poet—

> "She was a phantom of delight
> When first she gleamed upon my sight;
> A lovely apparition, sent
> To be a moment's ornament:
> Her eyes as stars of twilight fair,
> Like twilight, too, her dusky hair,
> But all things else about her drawn
> From Maytime and the cheerful dawn;
> A dancing shape, an image gay,
> To haunt, to startle, and waylay."

Nor was the accidental meeting without its effect upon Jessie Gray. On retiring to rest, she slept less soundly than usual, and in her dreams she was still falling into the river and being rescued by a stranger whose voice and features she could not recognize; and when she awoke in the morning, it was with that vague feeling of mental disquietude which stirring incidents or powerful emotions are apt to engender in the waking state before memory and consciousness have become fully aroused.

During the following day she could not refrain from speculating—she scarcely knew why—as to the possibility and probability of William Lyndsay again calling at Tifty. This might, of course, arise from strong feelings of gratitude; but when the young and impressive female heart becomes deeply stirred by such feelings towards one of the opposite sex, softer and gentler emotions rarely fail of following in their wake. Gratitude, sympathy, and deep interest are often the steps to the portico of the Temple of woman's love.

Jessie was not, however, kept very long in suspense, as nothing could be more natural or becoming on the part of William Lyndsay than that he should call to enquire after her welfare, seeing that the shock, though not severe, and the danger, though by no means very great, might have produced some ill results, even though temporary and trifling

Human nature is ever the same ; and, assuming on the part of two young people a disposition to meet each other, arguments as sound, as conclusive, and as logical, would have been found as readily in those days as in the present time, to shew the propriety of their so doing. Hence it requires no great straining of the imagination to suppose that the young people of whom we are speaking saw such necessity, recognized its importance, and faithfully and conscientiously acted up to their belief.

The acquaintance accidentally begun soon ripened into a warm attachment, and selecting as their trysting-place the Bridge of Skeugh, a romantic spot meetly chosen, they at length, in the face of the sunset heaven, whose one star stood as their witness, exchanged vows of mutual affection. Sometimes Steenie accompanied his sister, and at other times he would meet her on her way home.

It was not from a wish for concealment that Jessie did not at once mention her engagement to her father; she was waiting for Willie to speak first to Mr. Gray, and he intended to do so as soon as he returned from Montrose, whither he was going for a week or two to visit his father and mother. The young people never doubted that he would readily give his consent to their marriage.

About this time, and during the absence of Willie Lyndsay at Montrose, the father of Jessie being as yet in ignorance of his daughter's betrothal, it happened that the Laird of Fyvie, Sir Evan Seton, was one day riding past Tifty, when he saw Jessie standing at the door feeding her dog. Innocently bold and unconsciously beautiful, she shrank not from his gaze, but with a gentle smile and a respectful curtsey returned the Laird's salutation.

The contrast between the pretty simplicity of the maiden's attire, her lovely face and form, and the gaudy plumage of a peacock that was strutting up and down the grass plot in front of the house, proudly expanding his gorgeous tail in order to be admired, while she, as modest as she was attractive, seemed quite unconscious of the Laird's admiration, struck Sir Evan with astonishment; for he seldom came across beauty or youth, caring more for men's society, and rarely seeking that of the gentler sex. Now, however, he could not resist addressing Jessie, and soon found that she was the daughter of his tenant at Tifty.

Not many days elapsed ere Sir Evan again rode over the hill towards Tifty, on reaching which he was greatly disappointed at not seeing the same pretty face which he had so much admired on the former occasion. He now called at the farm and there saw Mr. Gray, who was much gratified by the Laird's condescension, and forthwith summoned his daughter to bring such refreshment as is usually and hospitably offered to visitors.

The extreme order and neatness everywhere apparent in the house, struck Sir Evan very forcibly; whilst the quiet simplicity, the graceful ease, and natural elegance of Jessie Gray, fed still further a flame that had been but too fiercely kindled at his first interview.

His visits to Tifty now became frequent, and believing himself to be in love, when a more subtle analysis of his feelings would have shown him but too clearly that his coarse nature was altogether insusceptible of that gentle passion, he determined on making Jessie his wife, not deeming it possible that any circumstances could lead her to reject his proposals.

And thus, before Willie Lyndsay's return, which from some unexplained cause had been delayed more than a month, Sir Evan Seton and Mr. Gray had arranged that Jessie should be the Lady of Fyvie.

Great was the consternation of Jessie when her father (never dreaming of any disinclination or opposition, on her part) imparted to her what he considered, the good news. She threw herself at his feet, and told him all that had passed between her and Willie Lyndsay, how great was their mutual affection, and also their intention of asking his consent to their union.

At this Gray became very wroth, declaring vehemently that he would rather follow her to the grave than see her married to William Lyndsay. He urged, nay, commanded, her to think no more of him; and in tones of authority from which there seemed to be no appeal, he told her to prepare for her marriage with the Laird, which should take place in the course of a few weeks.

Stunned and almost paralyzed by this communication, poor Jessie was well-nigh distracted. She implored her father to have pity on her, to remember her engagement to Willie, the cruelty to him as well as to herself if she set it aside, and more particularly the self-reproach that must inevitably follow; she moreover promised her father that she would not marry without his consent, if he, on his part, would desist from urging her to marry the Laird, of whom she knew so little, for whom she had not, and never could have, any affection, and whose position in life was so far beyond her own. Gray, somewhat relenting, bade her consider the matter when she had become more calm ; then, bidding her good night, left her to her own sorrowful musings.

Within a day or two Willie Lyndsay returned to Fyvie, and sent a message to Jessie to meet him as usual ; she did so, and told him all that had occurred during his absence. They hoped still to soften her father, and Willie left Jessie and went up to Tifty to see Mr. Gray if possible. He was fortunate in finding him at home. He told him of his love for Jessie, and having explained to him his prospects in life, which were very fair, and quite as good as any girl in Jessie's station could require, he proposed to marry her at once, if Mr. Gray would give his consent.

Gray, still dazzled by what he deemed the brilliant prospects of a marriage with the Laird of Fyvie, and with a fixed determination for its accomplishment, regardless of the sacrifice it would demand on the part of his daughter, gave an artful and evasive reply, so as to disarm Willie of all doubt as to his ultimate compliance. It is true he laid great stress on the circumstance of Jessie's youth, and suggested that it would be much better for them both if the marriage were delayed for a time; but he gave Willie no intimation of the existence of any obstacle to its eventual fulfilment.

Willie left Tifty in a very joyful state of mind, having good hope and trust in the future, and looking forward to a life of happiness with his dearly loved Jessie. Gray, however, told him he was not to meet her until he had seen him again, and Willie promised he would not seek her until he had received his answer.

The next morning Gray went to the Castle and had a long interview with the Laird, and when he left he was observed to be deadly pale.

When the day came for Willie Lyndsay to go to Tifty to receive his answer from Mr. Gray, he did not make his appearance; and two or three days having passed without any intelligence of him, Jessie was at a loss how to account for his absence, as, although she had not seen him since the day after his return, she had heard from her brother that he was to come to Tifty at that time to settle matters finally with her father.

Time passed on and the absence of Willie excited the wonder and aroused the suspicions of the neighbours; and at length a rumour became current that the Laird of Fyvie had been robbed, and that William Lyndsay was strongly suspected of being the culprit.

The circumstances attendant upon the robbery were such as to make it appear almost impossible that it could have been committed by any other person. And so strong was the evidence said to be against him, that rewards were offered for his apprehension.

Jessie was almost broken-hearted. She never for a moment suspected her lover, having the fullest trust in his honour and integrity; but alas! poor fellow, he was condemned on all sides; his absence, of course, being the principal cause of suspicion having fallen on him.

The property the Laird had lost, consisted of jewels, which were said to have been taken from a drawer in one of the small turrets off the library, to which William had access, when engaged, as he often was, in making up the estate accounts for the Laird. The key of the drawer was usually kept by the Laird; but at the time of the robbery the drawer was found unlocked, and the key on the floor of the passage leading from the library to the drawing-room.

The Laird did not hesitate to accuse the absent Willie, and expressed his determination to punish him as soon as he could be found.

Poor Jessie was borne down with grief and anxiety, as time rolled on, and there came no tidings of Willie. No one gave her comfort, no one offered her sympathy; she was doomed rather to have her sorrow aggravated and her affectionate heart still more wrung by the remarks of those around her, which not only expressed suspicion of Willie but conveyed reproach to herself, for bestowing so much thought upon, and displaying such anguish at the loss of, one altogether unworthy of her. Even her much loved brother Steenie could but condemn Willie, for, as he said justly enough, Where was he? Why did he not come to meet the accusation and justify himself, if he could? He said that, with every wish to think well of the young man, he considered it was a case full of suspicion, and he could not blame those who thought him guilty.

In sorrowful mood and in plaintive accents, Jessie would sometimes repeat, in a reverie of despair, these lines:—

> "But Willie's gone, whom I thought on,
>   And does not hear me weeping;
> Draws many a tear frae true love's ee
>   When other maids are sleeping.
>
> O came ye by yon waterside?
>   Pou'd you the rose or lily?
> Or came you by yon meadow green,
>   Or saw ye my sweet Willie?"

After a time the excitement in a measure subsided, and things returned to the usual routine at Tifty. Jessie was quiet and seemed more resigned, but she rarely smiled; her heart pleaded against her judgment in favour of her absent lover, as she could not believe him guilty, neither could she feel less warm affection for him.

Enquiries had been made at Montrose, where his friends resided, but nothing was heard of him there.

After the lapse of some weeks, Jessie's father softened in manner towards her, he spake more kindly, and studied to please her in every way; he also often complained of the times being bad and of having lost money; then again he would become quite lowspirited; but he never told her the reason of this, although Jessie often questioned him as to the cause.

His apparent grief and oppression at last became so great as to be altogether beyond any consolation which she could offer him, although her amiable and affectionate nature prompted her to do everything in her power which could have a tendency to withdraw his thoughts from some subject which was evidently causing him much mental distress. Her attentions to him were incessant, and bestowed with a gentleness and tact such as woman alone can display—characteristics which, appreciated by one of Caledonia's greatest sons, led him to apostrophize her in these well-known lines :—

> " When pain and anguish wring the brow,
> A ministering angel thou ! "

Taciturn, thoughtful, and moody, Gray caused his daughter much anxiety, and cast a deep gloom over the whole household ; but no word escaped his lips which could in any way lead his family to divine the cause of his distress.

It happened that having one day observed her father to be more silent and depressed than ever, Jessie watched him more closely and anxiously; and as she entered the parlour, where he usually sat of an evening and smoked his pipe before going to bed, she saw him sitting with his elbows on the table and his hands covering his face, evidently in deep thought. The slight noise she made on opening the door disturbed him, and as he looked up she saw that his eyes were filled with tears. At this sight, so unexpected, she started back, scarcely believing she saw clearly, so amazed was she on beholding her father, so little prone to the display of emotion of any kind, thus unmanned and overcome.

She felt that it must be a trial and trouble of no ordinary kind that could so move the strong and hard man to tears. The opportunity was now come, and she was not slow in availing herself of the occasion. Earnestly and affectionately, in the softest and most persuasive tones, she implored him to unburden his mind to her, so that she might at least share, if she could not mitigate, his grief.

With apparent reluctance and hesitation, Gray at length revealed the secret that seemed to have been grieving him, obtaining relief to his over-wrought feelings, as he narrated to his daughter the sad history of his difficulties, his humiliation, and his crime.

Having, he said, without the knowledge of his family, engaged in a speculation which eventually proved to be a disastrous failure, he had been called upon to pay a considerable sum of money, which he had not at his command. In this strait, and in an evil hour, without considering the consequences of his act, he forged the signature of Sir Evan Seton to a bill to meet the emergency, intending and hoping that he would be able to obtain money to redeem the bill before it came to maturity, and so to avoid all possible likelihood of its falling into the hands of the Laird. Most unfortunately for him, however, he said the friend who held this document, so perilous to his reputation and his life, had died suddenly, and the note being found by his family, had already been transmitted to the Laird, who now held it in his possession. Gray then further explained to his daughter the nature of the crime of which he had been guilty, and the penalty attaching thereto.

He moreover assured her that Sir Evan Seton had the power to prosecute him, and not only the power, but the will also, in which case he could expect no mercy, for he was quite certain none would be shown, and it would only remain for him to expiate his crime by an ignominious death.

Sir Evan, he said, had of late shown unmistakeable signs of displeasure towards himself and his family, and amongst these his protracted absence from Tifty was not the least significant.

Jessie's grief was indeed very great, and it was some time before she recovered sufficiently to speak to her poor father, with whom she deeply sympathized, for although he was not a tender father, still he was never actually unkind, and had always appeared to love her better than anyone else in the world. She also felt for him, in that it must have caused him shame, deep and abiding, in having to confess his guilt to his own child.

When she was able to speak to him, she urged him to go to the Castle the next day and endeavour to see the Laird, and, if possible, persuade him to spare him the ignominy of a public exposure; and at the same time to assure him that he would sell all that he had in order to make up the money to pay the amount of the bill, if Sir Evan would only forbear from prosecuting him for the forgery. Gray promised his child that he would do what she suggested, and they then parted for the night; but, alas! there could be no sleep for poor Jessie.

She was quite overwhelmed with grief; her father's dishonour coming so quickly upon the mysterious absence of Willie Lyndsay added so much to her burden as to render it almost too grievous to be borne. Until now she had been able to attend cheerfully to her daily duties in managing the household affairs. Believing fully in the innocence of Willie, and feeling daily more and more convinced of the utter impossibility of his having committed the crime laid to his charge, she was becoming in some degree reconciled to his absence, by the hope that he would ere long return to her, triumphantly refute his accusers, and give a satisfactory explanation of his disappearance.

She had read of separations even longer than theirs, attended with most romantic incidents, and ending with the restoration of the missing one to his friends: she trusted that a similar fate might befal Willie and herself; and, although the elasticity of her step and the buoyancy of her spirits had by no means returned, her sorrow was subdued, and the dark cloud that overshadowed her had become less dark and was fringed with the silvery rays that harbingered the dawn of hope.

But now had come this terrible revelation of her father, saddening still more her youthful heart, and bowing her down with shame and disgrace. Here was no room for hope—no possibility of an unforeseen and happy termination to her suspense—inasmuch as her father had confessed his crime, and nothing could alter its gravity or lessen the dishonour that attached to it.

The next day Gray went to the Castle to see the Laird, who, being at the time engaged, sent a message telling him to call again at six o'clock that evening. At the appointed hour he returned to the Castle, and obtained an audience with Sir Evan Seton. From this interview he appeared to have derived no comfort or satisfaction, for on reaching his home he was still dejected and silent; he seemed even more unhappy than before, and his countenance wore the aspect of hopeless despair. Not a word escaped him as to the result of his visit to the Castle; but, on parting with his daughter for the night, he intimated to her his intention of telling her on the following day all that had passed between him and the Laird. There was, however, no opportunity during the next day for Jessie and her father to have any confidential conversation, her brother Steenie being at home, and Gray had desired Jessie to observe the same secrecy towards him as to the others, telling her he would not live if he were disgraced in the eyes of his sons.

When night came and they were all retiring to rest, Gray whispered to his daughter to return to him in the course of half an hour. She did so, and after much hesitation he imparted to her that he had had great difficulty in persuading the Laird to listen to him at all; and when he at length did so, and had heard his (Gray's) earnest petition for forgiveness, he replied at once that on one condition only would he pardon him—that condition being that he should give him his daughter in marriage; and he now, therefore. appealed to her to give her consent to an union so brilliant and advantageous to herself, and fraught with such weighty consequences to himself—consequences involving no less an issue than life or death.

Jessie wept bitterly for a time. Her emotion was most painful to behold, her whole frame being convulsed with the terrible struggle to subdue and subordinate her own feelings to her father's wishes. At length, however, she so far yielded submission as to say she would marry Sir Evan, provided she could do so without wronging another; adding that if Willie Lyndsay were living, no power on earth should induce her to break her plighted troth; no artifice, no temptation, should lead her to marry another. And as for the worldly advantages which might result to her from her marriage with Sir Evan, she esteemed them lightly as compared with the bright and solid happiness that attended upon those unions wherein heart was given for heart, and soul reflected back to soul its purest, holiest feelings.

Her father urged her more and more, and she then said that if she were quite certain of the fate of Willie she would sacrifice her own happiness to save her father from the ruin that threatened him.

Gray replied that this was but a profession of generosity and a pretence of caring for her poor father; as it must be evident to everyone that William Lyndsay was gone from Fyvie altogether, and that there could be no doubt of his having taken the missing property, which would render his return impossible.

Gray used every argument to overcome his child's scruples, and eventually succeeded. Her soft and tender heart melted at the sight of her father's grief, and her fear for his life induced her to consent to his wishes, on condition that Sir Evan Seton would at once destroy the dangerous document, and that he would be content with her respect and obedience, and not expect from her the affection she could not give. She would endeavour, she said, to do her duty; more she could not promise.

Gray was profuse in his thanks to, and praises of, his daughter, and expatiated at some length upon the advantages of her future position; she however sadly replied, "What was the use of fine silken gowns with a poor, broken heart?"

There was nothing in the manners or personal appearance of Sir Evan Seton calculated to win the affections of a young girl.

In age about forty, tall, bony and gaunt, with red or rather dark sandy hair, a rough voice, and an eye that never met another's, overshadowed by bushy overhanging eyebrows, all combined to produce an aspect repulsive rather than attractive, and which indicated an absence of refined tastes and feelings, and afforded but too clearly an index to a cold, selfish, and impulsive nature. He was well known to be of an irascible temper, and of a morose and vindictive disposition — characteristics which were such as to augur no very bright prospect or hopes of happiness for Jessie Gray, who felt throughout it all, that—

> " It's no in titles nor in rank,
>   It's no in wealth like Lon'on bank,
>   To purchase peace and rest;
>   It's no in making muckle mair,
>   It's no in books, it's no in lear,
>   To make us truly blest:
>   If happiness hae not her seat
>   And centre in the breast,
>   We may be wise, or rich, or great,
>   But never can be blest:
>   Nae treasures, nor pleasures,
>   Could make us happy long;
>   The heart ay's the part ay,
>   That makes us right or wrong."

The next day Gray informed his family of

the approaching marriage of Jessie to the Laird of Fyvie. With the exception of Steenie (who knew that his sister's heart was not in the marriage) they were much pleased at the idea, and thought at once of the many benefits they would derive from their sister becoming a great lady.

In a short time the wedding took place quietly at Tifty. At the Castle there were great rejoicings.

> " So they were wed, and merrily rang the bells,
> Merrily rang the bells, and they were wed,
> But never merrily beat Jessie's heart.
> A footstep seemed to fall beside her path,
> She knew not whence; a whisper in her ear,
> She knew not what; nor loved she to be left
> Alone at home, nor ventured out alone."

Jessie—or, as we should now call her, the Lady of Fyvie—endeavoured in all ways to please her husband. She consulted his wishes in everything, and by her patient submission ought to have preserved his love; but his was not a nature to be easily restrained by either a sense of duty or by the wishes of others; nor was it likely that it would long be held in subjection by the silken chains of an affection that had far more in it of earth than heaven.

Time passed wearily on, and with the wings of its flight it fanned in vain the dying embers of Sir Evan's passion. Two or three years were sufficient for the steady growth of a cruel and cold indifference, which soon ripened into a studied and almost contemptuous neglect, so that there remained to the poor Lady of Fyvie scarcely even the small consolation contained in the well-known lines :—

" He will hold thee when his passion shall have spent its
    novel force ;
Something better than his dog, a little dearer than his
    horse."

Sustained by a strong sense of duty and the conscientious fulfilment of the promise made at the time of her marriage, Jessie repined not at her lot, but silently, though sorrowfully, submitted herself to her husband's will, endured his caprices, and murmured not at his indignities. Feelings of self-reproach would, at times, almost prompt her to see in her trials and vexations instances of avenging justice; and then her grief became excessive, and she experienced with an intensity that agitated to a great degree her whole frame and almost set her brain on fire,

> " That a sorrow's crown of sorrow is remembering happier things."

Shipwrecked on the rock of her father's ambition, toiling in the meshes of an alliance from which she could not escape, Jessie's health began to fail under the continual sorrow and disappointment that had now fallen to her lot.

Gray saw with alarm and with many a pang of deep regret the change that had come over his daughter; and the knowledge that she was so cruelly neglected by her husband so embittered his existence and harassed his mind that he became seriously ill; and so great was his mental and bodily prostration, he was scarcely expected to recover from his illness.

For some time prior to this Sir Evan Seton had studiously striven to prevent any frequent or private interviews between his wife and her father, prompted to this course by various motives.

Having grown weary of his wife, and become more alive to the inferiority of her position before her marriage, the society of her relations was now positively irksome to him; and with a bitterness characteristic of weak minds, that seek in the artificial exaltation of rank and the fleeting vanities of title a compensation for manly feelings and the nobler virtues, he let pass no opportunity of wounding and humiliating them by an affection of superiority and a supercilious disdainful neglect, unmindful that "'Tis only noble to be good."

It happened, however, at the time of Mr. Gray's illness, and when he was reduced to a state of great weakness, that Sir Evan was called from home to attend the funeral of a neighbouring proprietor; and during his absence, which extended over some hours, Lady Seton hastened to pay a visit to her father at Tifty. He was much pleased to see her, and greeted her warmly; her presence seemed to have a calming influence upon the suffering and troubled man. He appeared to be endowed with renewed vigour; and after the first few moments were passed, he lay for a long time silently contemplating with an expression of deep anxiety and sorrow the still beautiful face of his much loved child—a face so calmly sweet that its soft beauty still shone through the clouds of trouble and despair that had overshadowed it, even as the pale cold Queen of Night shines forth in full glory and loveliness from amidst her cloudy canopy.

With heated brain, nerves racked, and mind tortured almost beyond endurance, Gray at length summoned to his aid such a degree of self-control and resolution as enabled him to unburden himself of the sad secret that had so long bound him down, and was now but too surely thrusting him into his grave.

Having first made his daughter promise never to reveal what he was going to tell her, he slowly, earnestly, and solemnly craved her forgiveness for the sin he had sinned, and which had caused her such dire distress; and not her only, but himself also, and for which repentance had now, alas! come too late.

In faltering tones and broken accents he confessed to her that he had been instrumental in practising upon her a cruel and gross fraud, in which falsehood, deception, and ambition had each played its respective part. He told her that by a concerted plan between Sir Evan Seton and himself, William Lyndsay had been removed from his home and placed elsewhere in seclusion, and secured from all chance of escape; moreover, that the story of the robbery at the Castle and William's supposed guilt was an entire fabrication, as was also that of his own alleged forgery of Sir Evan's name; all of which falsehoods had been invented for the sole purpose of weaning her affection from William, and inducing her to consent to marry the Laird.

This revelation cost Gray many pangs of remorse, and well nigh crushed poor Jessie with a grief too intense for expression, too deep to be washed away in tears.

Having made to his child this mortifying

confession, Gray, quite exhausted with the excitement, became unconscious; and, although he rallied again for a time, he lived but a few days longer, and then died a victim to remorse and the pangs of a guilty conscience. Whether he might have felt differently had he seen his daughter happy cannot now be known; but there is no doubt it added very much to the acuteness of his feelings of wretchedness when he saw how completely her life was wrecked and wasted, and that in all probability death would ere long claim in her another victim to his wicked machinations.

To the poor Lady Seton, already so subdued in spirit and broken in health, this addition to her misery seemed to fill to overflowing her cup of sorrow. To have been so cruelly deceived by her own father was a dreadful thing to contemplate. No reproaches fell from her lips: reproaches then being powerless for averting or mitigating the sad train of miseries which had been the fruits of his deception.

Then again her heart was lacerated with agonies of doubt and terror respecting the fate of poor Willie Lyndsay. He might still be living; and even know of her marriage, and, being ignorant of the circumstances that led to that ill-fated union, be pouring forth from the depth of his wounded spirit invectives against her faithless and heartless conduct. Or worse even than this, the same treachery and wickedness that prompted his removal from the neighbourhood, might have sanctioned a greater crime, and he may have suffered for his deep and sincere affection for her, a premature and violent death.

In silence and despair she bore her grievous afflictions; from her husband, a participator in the guilt of her father, she could expect no sympathy, neither might it be consistent with his own safety to make any revelations respecting the fate of William Lyndsay.

To whom then could she turn? Happily for her, the peace, and hope, and consolations of the religion inculcated in her early years now shone forth in even greater glory, and she turned for comfort to that precious volume whose sacred pages record the weepings and wailings of troubled hearts like her own, and reveal the sympathy and boundless mercy of a loving Saviour, who has tenderly addressed his suffering children in these beautiful and compassionate words, " Come unto me all ye that labour and are heavy laden, and I will give you rest."

Her sorrow became subdued, and a holy calm took possession of her mind, which her deep and abiding grief seldom disturbed. There appeared to have passed over her sad spirit a heavenly influence that soothed her melancholy and softened her despair.

Sir Evan Seton was much relieved by the death of Gray, and as the lease of Tifty had nearly expired, he offered to take the farm into his own occupation at once in lieu of past rents, and having completed this arrangement and provided for the sons, by obtaining for them suitable situations at a distance, he considered that he had quite done his duty towards the brothers of his wife, and what was still more important, he had ensured as he hoped, their absence from Fyvie altogether, or at least during the lifetime of Jessie.

The parting between the brothers and sister was very painful, particularly when Jessie came to say farewell to Steenie, for she had never contemplated such a complete isolation from all who were dear to her, but had hoped for the comfort of sometimes seeing him, trusting that employment would be found for him near home, if not at Fyvie; he was, however, destined to go to Ireland, and she could not expect to see him often, if ever again.

Slowly now the time crept on, and the Lady of Fyvie became paler and thinner from day to day; everbody pitied her, and felt for the interesting young being whose life was so sad and blighted. Her manner, always pleasing and attractive, indicated a full appreciation of the kindness of the ladies of her neighbourhood, with whom she associated and exchanged friendly visits, as often as her failing health would allow her to do; she also felt a degree of gratitude for what she deemed their condescension, inasmuch as she had the good sense to see and acknowledge that her accidental elevation by marriage could not obliterate those social distinctions which will ever prevail between those who are born and cradled in the lap of luxury and extravagance, and those who, by no means less useful, less honourable, or less worthy, are of humble origin and defective education.

Sad, yet uncomplaining; wronged, yet not reproachful; suffering, but not repining; she could not fail to awaken in the minds of all who beheld her, a deep interest and heart-felt pity. Her neighbours evinced towards her the warmest sympathy, some of them with a gentleness and tenderness peculiar to those who possess that good-breeding which contents itself not with fashionable display, affected superiority, and supercilious impertinence, but which exalts the individual by ennobling the heart.

Alas! it was but too apparent that the outward calm did not extend to the troubled waters of the spirit, which were agitated daily by a sense of cruel wrongs and studied neglect from her husband. It was quite clear that the fragile frame of poor Lady Seton could not long sustain this contest, and there were already indications of failing health and strength. The symptoms increased rapidly, and she soon became so weak and feeble, that although no palpable disease had proclaimed itself, it was but too evident her life was ebbing away.

Doctor MacGreg, whose opinion had been sought by her own medical attendant and friend, Mr. Mackie, confirmed the unfavourable report of the latter, and expressed his conviction that no human aid could avail to save, or even much prolong her life. In this extremity medical skill could do no more than point out the course which humanity alone would dictate, viz., to alleviate her sufferings, to calm her mind, and to smooth as far as possible her pathway to the grave. Doctor MacGreg and Mr. Mackie, with decision and firmness, urged upon Sir Evan Seton the duty and necessity of adopting all their recommendations, nor were they, although irritated and disgusted by his apathy and cold indifference, deterred from taking decisive steps to secure their observance.

They insisted on the propriety of sending at once for Lady Seton's brothers, as a duty to them and in fulfilment of her own earnestly expressed wishes. Fortunately some delay had occurred in the departure of Steenie from the country, and he was, therefore, enabled promptly to obey the summons to attend upon his dying sister—at least, as soon as the capricious and vacillating Laird would allow a messenger to be despatched to Aberdeen for him, which was not until after the lapse of some days.

This cruel delay had nearly accomplished the object of the Laird, for Steenie on his arrival found his sister so ill and exhausted that it was with difficulty she could converse with him. He was deeply affected by her appearance, her sunken features and pallid cheek, her expression of painful languor, yet of deep resignation, and her beautiful dark eyes softly radiant with unwonted lustre, lighting up as it were the wreck of her former loveliness, like the warm glow of sun-set upon some beautiful ruin.

His presence had a great effect upon his sister; the pleasure which she experienced tended to rouse her flagging powers, and she revived sufficiently to be enabled to converse a little with him. The Laird, who was in the adjoining room, would not allow the brother and sister to have too long a private interview, and, therefore, soon interrupted them, and brought in with him the Doctors, who had just arrived at the Castle. At the moment they entered the room, Jessie said, in a clear though subdued tone, which was heard by all, "Dear Steenie, I shall never rest until my poor Willie's bones have Christian burial."

The Laird started violently, but recovering himself quickly he exclaimed, "Poor thing! poor thing! quite delirious!" In the course of a few minutes the Lady of Fyvie passed away, as quietly as if she were sleeping.

The death of his wife, though for some reasons and in some degree a relief, appeared at first to subdue in a measure the obdurate nature of Sir Evan Seton; not that he gave way to any very marked demonstration of feeling; the supposition of his grief was rather an inference derived from his softer tones, his musing taciturnity, and his quiet acceptance of the customary and decorous retirement which the melancholy event imposed. It would be difficult to analyse the emotions that were stirring within him, as

> "His dark impassive face was cold as bronze ;
> His mouth locked up in silence like a chest
> Whose key is lost, or drawn as it had worn

A life-long curb; his forehead full and bare,
Where not a wrinkle told what passed within.
Sometimes his hands would twitch when he was moved,
But not his lips, no, nor his cold round eyes,
From which he shut all meaning at his will."

It would, however, be judging human nature too hardly, to suppose that he did not feel a sincere, though it might prove but a transient sorrow for the loss of his wife; and we cannot but suppose that some feelings of regret and remorse for the neglect and unkindness with which he had of late treated her, must have been awakened even in his hard heart.

His grief may have been none the less sincere, though feebly demonstrative; it may have been, it is true, too much

" Like a snowflake on the river,
    A moment seen then gone for ever."

For there are natures whose depths are stirred only by the fiercer passions and ruder feelings, and which scarcely yield a ripple to the gentler emotions and sympathies which agitate deeply more sensitive minds.

Still to all, death is an awful presence; and in his presence we are led to reflections calculated to soften the hardest heart; and it is probable that in his retirement, Sir Evan Seton may have yielded to, perhaps have been appalled by, such meditations.

His implacable and imperious nature would have refused, however, to allow even a look, a word, or a gesture to betray the circumstance of his having been agitated by any such solemn thoughts, as his natural pride would have prohibited him from manifesting to those around him any degree of sorrowful repentance. There was that in his general demeanour which indicated more or less restlessness; and rumour, with its hundred tongues, was not slow in assigning causes for his disquietude.

It was whispered about that he could not

sleep soundly as heretofore, that his rest was disturbed by perplexing dreams, and that his dead wife sometimes appeared to him.

On one occasion, his servants were suddenly aroused by screams proceeding from his room, upon entering which, they found him very much excited, and in an almost fainting state from the violence of his emotion. He soon recovered his self-possession, and abruptly told them that he was subject to attacks of nightmare; at the same time, however, he devised some expedient for retaining his personal attendant about him for the remainder of the night.

But whatever may have been the measure of his grief or the depth of his remorse, Time, " the consumer of all things," brought with it in its flight, changes of feeling and of circumstances, and at no very distant period from the death of Lady Seton, Sir Evan had returned to his former associates, and to his habits of revelry and dissipation. Living in troublous times, when faction was rife, and a rebellious spirit only too general, his turbulent disposition but too readily prompted him to take part with the disloyal and disaffected, and without any palpable cause or plausible excuse for his disloyalty, he became an active and prominent enemy of the sovereign, and made no secret of his rebellious designs.

At length he and his adherents drew upon themselves the notice of the Government, and it required but little investigation to satisfy the authorities of their treasonable purposes. Arrests were made, but fortunately for Sir Evan, on the very day on which a detachment of troops arrived at Fyvie to accomplish his capture, he had departed for Edinburgh for the purpose of having an interview with one of the principal leaders of what was intended to be a formidable revolt. On his way thither intelligence accidentally reached him of the arrest and imprisoment of several of his colleagues, and he then saw his own perilous position. With all practicable speed he hastened on to Edinburgh, where he was but little known, as the distance at which he resided, and the difficulties that attended travelling in those days, precluded the possibility of frequent visits to the metropolis of Scotland.

On his arrival, he at once gained the fullest information respecting the arrests, and, knowing how deeply he was implicated, he thought it prudent to seek safety in immediate flight from his country. With all possible expedition he sought out the nearest point for embarkation, and from thence set sail for the Continent, leaving for ever the home of his childhood and the country of his birth. His castle and lands were confiscated. We care not to follow him in his subsequent career; we may, however, express a charitable hope that ere too late he repented of his former wicked life.

After the departure of Sir Evan Seton, strange rumours went abroad, and the old Castle became invested with additional interest to many, and with terror to not a few. It was currently reported, and generally believed, that Sir Evan Seton had seen the Ghost of Fyvie, that the servants had often heard strange noises, and had seen shadows passing along the walls, and that there was not one among the inmates of the Castle who would have ventured to go on the great staircase after dark. When asked to give a reason for their superstitious fears, they would reply, "She walks at night troubled;" and so it came to be rumoured that a fair young lady, clad in green silk, walked up and down the staircase and along the passages at night, more often during the winter, but always between the hours of eleven and one!

Years rolled on, and the fine old Castle saw the entrance and the exit of several proprietors, some of them being a blessing to the neighbourhood in which they dwelt, using their possessions with benevolence and liberality, conscious of the important trust and high privileges that had devolved upon them, whilst others almost rivalled Sir Evan Seton in selfishness and recklessness. At length the Fyvie property descended to Mr. Murray, a young man calculated in every way to exalt the position to which he had attained, instead of trusting to that position for his own elevation.

Young, energetic, captivating, and chivalrous, we may feel assured that his noble and generous heart was tenderly susceptible of the influence of female beauty and grace, and that his taste, chaste and refined, would lead him to select for his wife one worthy of his admiration and his love. Such was the case, and, probably, no where could be found a more beautiful place, or more happy occupants. Their charities were freely dispensed, their hospitality was almost unbounded, and yet so quietly and unostentatiously displayed that it warmed the heart without chilling the spirits.

They had not been long at Fyvie when rumours of a ghost story reached the ears of Mrs. Murray, and amused her exceedingly. She at first paid but little attention to the absurd tale, but seeing that it had evidently made a strong impression upon the minds of many of her household, she began to think it necessary to take more serious notice of it.

Now, it is quite true, that in a warm, comfortable, well-lighted drawing-room, with numerous friends about us, conversation lively, wit sparkling, vivacity reigning everywhere around, we may listen to a ghost story with amusement, and preserve the tranquillity of our nerves and the serenity of our mind undisturbed; but to occupy the same house with a ghost, to know its haunts, its shape, even its colour, to move about with the stillness of night, with the expectation, nay, almost certainty, of meeting *him*, *her*, or *it*, is a very different thing, and many a hero or heroine of a drawing-room would, under these circumstances, be found wanting in their previously-boasted courage.

It has never yet been proved that there are not ghosts, why, therefore, should there be such a degree of incredulity respecting their existence? At all events it will be found invariably to be the case, that our incredulity diminishes in inverse proportion to our propinquity to a ghost.

So it was with Mrs. Murray; she felt a little uncomfortable if her husband was detained from home at night, and she then moved about from room to room rather cautiously, casting a suspicious look here and there; and, with her imagination deeply impressed as it was, it required but the disturbing influence of a late supper to have furnished her with as complete and satisfactory a ghost as probably human eyes have ever beheld. She would not exactly allow that she was afraid of a ghost, although she could not deny that she had vague and indescribable feelings of discomfort closely allied to fear, the cause for which she could not altogether assign.

One night when Mr. Murray was absent from home, Janet, Mrs. Murray's waiting-maid, rushed into her mistress's room, pale with fright, and for some minutes unable to utter a word; at last she gasped out that she had seen the Green Ladye! She could say nothing more, could give no description of what she had seen, could not say what the Green Ladye was like, and simply repeated over and over again that she had passed her. Mrs. Murray was rather alarmed at the excited state of her maid, and thought it advisable to desire her to sleep in her room that night, more for the sake of the girl than for any comfort or protection for herself, although she could not help being a little agitated at what had occurred.

The next morning Mrs. Murray inquired of Mrs. Milne, the housekeeper, what was the report in connection with the ghost, what was its foundation, and whether she or any of the other servants had seen or heard anything extraordinary or unusual at any time.

Mrs. Milne told her that since she had been at the Castle, she had never thought of anything of the kind, but that sometimes the younger servants joked each other about the Green Ladye, and probably they might have been speaking of the ghost before Janet, the waiting-maid, and in consequence of this, she may have fancied that she heard or saw something.

Mrs. Milne then related the story of the unfortunate Lady Seton, and said that credulous people imagined she walked about the staircase and passages at night; she also told her of the tradition of the last words of Lady Seton. Mrs. Murray was much shocked at this, and asked Mrs. Milne a great many questions; when the housekeeper seeing how much her mistress was interested in all she said about those old times, mentioned to her that there was a sealed chamber in the Castle, situated under the Charter-room, and that no one knew what it contained, the general supposition being that a quantity of treasure was concealed there. Mrs. Murray immediately exclaimed, that as soon as her husband returned, of course he would order the room to be examined. The housekeeper then said, she trusted her mistress would not urge Mr. Murray to attempt to open this secret place, as it was fully believed that if it were opened, nothing would ever again prosper at the Castle, or at least during the lifetime of the proprietor in possession at the time, and she hoped that Mrs. Murray would not be the means of bringing such a calamity upon herself and her husband.

Mrs. Murray was not to be diverted from her purpose, and her curiosity was so greatly excited that on the return of her husband she persuaded him that it was quite essential to her happiness, nay, to her health, that she should know what really was in this mysterious chamber.

Mr. Murray demurred for a while, but unable long to resist the entreaties of his wife, eventually consented to gratify her curiosity, and in the presence of the steward and other servants and dependants, and of two or three friends who were at the time visiting at the Castle, the dreaded investigation took place.

It was then discovered to be, not a chamber, but a dungeon! Lights were brought, and to the horror and amazement of the assembled party, they saw that the cell contained a skeleton which had partially mouldered away; the remains of a man, which must have been concealed there for many years. They also found by the side of the skeleton, an earthen pitcher, a trumpet, and a curious stone, which last was quite wet, although the cell was simply damp as a dungeon would be.

One of the old retainers exclaimed, surely this must be the skeleton of Willie Lyndsay, an accountant and trumpeter, who mysteriously disappeared in the time of one of the former Lairds. Others then joined in the conversation, and it soon became quite clear that the young man William Lyndsay must have been foully murdered by Sir Evan Seton, and that the story of his having robbed him, had, no doubt, been invented to account for his disappearance; this was further corroborated by the discovery on the trumpet of the initials W. L.; some one now remembered and repeated the last words of the unfortunate Lady Seton, "I shall never rest until my poor Willie's bones have Christian burial."

In the course of a few days the remains of this ill-fated victim were buried in the kirkyard of Fyvie, and the dungeon was then closed as before.

Mrs. Milne was much troubled when she found that all her efforts to dissuade Mrs. Murray from having the chamber opened, had been in vain, and that her mistress shrank not from the risk of any misery she might bring on herself or her husband, but when year after year passed away without bringing upon them any untoward calamity or misfortune, she was fairly puzzled, and could never satisfactorily account to herself for their immunity from the consequences of the fatal act.

After a time, Mr. Murray caused a figure to be made to represent the trumpeter, and had it placed on the highest part of the Preston Tower, where it may now be seen pointing the silent trumpet towards Tifty. Whether the Green Ladye is now ever seen or heard moving restlessly along the passages, can only be known to the inmates of the Castle; but, this little history would probably by this time be quite forgotten, were it not for the tears constantly shed by the old stone, which is still preserved in one of the upper chambers of the Castle, and which ceases not to weep for the tragic fate of Jessie and Willie.

THE END.

Printed by RANKEN & Co., Drury House, St. Mary-le-Strand.

CPSIA information can be obtained at www.ICGtesting.com
Printed in the USA
LVOW110052140113

315553LV00004B/89/P